Active Meditations for Contemplative Prayer

· THOMAS KEATING ·

Active Meditations for Contemplative Prayer

continuum

NEW YORK · LONDON

The Continuum International Publishing Group Inc
80 Maiden Lane, New York, NY 10038

The Continuum International Publishing Group Ltd
The Tower Building, 11 York Road, London SE1 7NX

www.continuumbooks.com

The selections in this book are taken from the following books
of Thomas Keating: *The Heart of the World*, © 1981 by
Cistercian Abbey of St. Joseph; *Open Mind, Open Heart*, ©
1986, 1992 by St. Benedict's Monastery; *Crisis of Faith, Crisis of
Love*, © 1995 by St. Benedict's Monastery; *Invitation to Love*, ©
1992 by St. Benedict's Monastery.

Printed in the United States of America

Library of Congress Cataloging-in-Publication Data
Keating, Thomas.
Active meditations for contemplative prayer / Thomas
Keating.
p. cm.
ISBN 978-0-8264-2821-9 (paperback : alk. paper)
ISBN 0-8264-1061-8 (hardcover)
I.   Contemplation. 2. Meditations. I. Title.
        BV5091.C7K4   1997
    248.34 – dc214   97-39582

                                        CIP

Contents

Foreword

This compilation of quotes from the books of Thomas Keating is a welcome offering which will certainly make the essence of his work more accessible in a very convenient yet traditional form. Though Abbot Keating writes in a clear, incandescent style, seeing his work excerpted here in an aphoristic form makes one aware of how distinct a voice and vision his books offer. We are indebted to Grace Padilla, Billie Trinidad, Lita Salinas, and Contemplative Outreach, Philippines, for their work in making this compilation.

The quotations are drawn from a series of books through which Thomas Keating offers teaching on the method of Centering Prayer and its effects in daily life. To see these aphorisms expanded and fully developed in context, one should turn to Keating's principal works: *Open Mind, Open Heart*, the "how to" of Centering Prayer. Its sister volume, *Invitation to Love*, is a distillation of the contemplative dimension of the spiritual journey, the "what happens" as one grows in a prayer pratice such as Centering Prayer. *Intimacy with God* breaks new ground in bridging the gap between Christian contemplation, the contemporary sciences, paricularly psychology, and the other world religions. *The Mystery of Christ* and subsequent volumes, *Awakenings*, *Reawakenings*, and *The*

Kingdom of God Is Like. . . , are scripturally based meditations on the contemplative dimension of the Gospel. They elegantly substantiate the fact that Centering Prayer is distinctly Christian, grounded in Scripture, and is itself a distinct approach to Christian contemplation. These volumes were written as a series, and to understand the fullness of Thomas Keating's vision of the renewal of the contemplative dimension of the Gospel, they should be considered as a whole.

An application of this compilation is using it as a "minute book," a recommendation of Father Keating's. He suggests one carry a minute book in pocket or purse, a "series of short readings—a sentence or two, or at most a short paragraph—from your favorite spiritual writers or from your own journal that reminds you of your commitment to Christ and to contemplative prayer." In the midst of a busy day, when one finds a "stray minute or two," Keating recommends reading a few lines and reflecting. This book constitutes a splendid minute book for those for whom Keating's writings are both inspiration and guide. Keep it by your bedside, or near the chair where you observe your Centering Prayer period, even tuck it into a shopping bag or briefcase.

Gustave Reininger

ONE

Contemplation
Contemplative,
Prayer

What is the essence of contemplative prayer? The way of pure faith. Nothing else. You do not have to feel it, but you have to practice it.

Open Mind Open Heart p. 11

[*C*ontemplative prayer is the world in which] . . . our private, self-made worlds come to an end; a new world appears within and around us and the impossible becomes an everyday experience. Yet the world that prayer reveals is barely noticeable in the ordinary course of events.

Open Mind Open Heart p. 13

Contemplative prayer is not so much the absence of thoughts as detachment from them. It is the opening of mind and heart, body and emotions—our whole being—to God, the Ultimate Mystery, beyond words, thoughts and emotions.

    🪷 *Open Mind Open Heart p. 14*

*C*ontemplative prayer is the world in which God can do anything. . . . It is to be open to the Infinite and hence to infinite possibilities.

              ❧ *Open Mind Open Heart p. 13*

$\mathcal{T}$he quality of prayer rather than its quantity is what matters. A single moment of divine union is more valuable than a long period of prayer during which you are constantly in and out of interior silence. It only takes a moment for God to enrich you.

        ❦ *Open Mind Open Heart p. 57*

The desire to go to God, to open to His presence within us, does not come from our initiative. We do not have to go anywhere to find God because He is already drawing us in every conceivable way into union with Himself. It is rather a question of opening to an action that is already happening in us.

Open Mind Open Heart p. 46

$\mathcal{T}$his much is certain, that once we make up our minds to seek God, he is already seeking us much more eagerly, and he is not going to let anything happen to prevent his purpose.

Heart of the World p.41

$\mathcal{L}$ife . . . in union with God . . . is full of surprises. You can be sure whatever you expect to happen will not happen. That is the only thing of which you can be certain in the spiritual journey.

Open Mind Open Heart p. 105

· T W O ·

Centering Prayer

Centering prayer is not so much an exercise of attention as intention. It may take a while to grasp this distinction. You do not attend to any particular thought content. Rather, you *intend* to go to your inmost being, where you believe God dwells. You are opening to Him by pure faith, not by means of concepts or feelings.

     Open Mind Open Heart p. 39

[Centering prayer] is . . . a journey into the unknown. It is a call to follow Jesus out of all the structures, security blankets, and even spiritual practices that serve as props. They are all left behind insofar as they are part of the false self system. . . . False self is an illusion. It is our way of conceiving who we are and what the world is.

      🪷 *Open Mind Open Heart p. 72*

$\mathcal{A}$s your sensitivity to the spiritual dimension of your being develops through the daily practice of this [centering] prayer, you may begin to find the awareness of God's presence arising at times in ordinary activity. You may feel called to turn interiorly to God without knowing why. The quality of your spiritual life is developing and enabling you to pick up vibrations from a world you did not previously perceive. Without deliberately thinking of God, you may find that He is often present in the midst of your daily occupations.

        ❦ *Open Mind Open Heart p. 37*

*C*entering prayer is a method of refining one's intuitive faculties so that one can enter more easily into contemplative prayer. It is not the only path to contemplation, but it is a good one. As a method, it is a kind of extract to monastic spirituality . . . you have to keep up a certain level of interior silence in the psyche and nervous system if you want to obtain the benefits of contemplative prayer.

       Open Mind Open Heart p. 34

Pure faith will bring you closer to God than anything else. To be attached to an experience of God is not God; it is a thought. The time of centering prayer is the time to let go of all thoughts, even the best of thoughts. If they are really good, they will come back later.

Open Mind Open Heart p. 57

*I*f you overdo anything, it is bound to have some bad side effects. Too much joy as well as too much sorrow is fatiguing. The purpose of this prayer is not more prayer or more silence, but the integration of prayer and silence with activity.

        ❦ *Open Mind Open Heart p. 65*

· THREE ·

Thoughts

Our ordinary preoccupations involve unconscious value systems. Some thoughts are attractive to us because we have an attachment to them springing from the emotional programming of early childhood. When such thoughts go by, all our lights start flashing because of our heavy emotional investment in the values that they stimulate or threaten. By training ourselves to let go of every thought and thought pattern, we gradually develop freedom from our attachments and compulsions.

           Open Mind Open Heart p. 45

Denial of our inmost self includes detachment from the habitual functioning of our intellect and will, which are our inmost faculties. This may require letting go not only of ordinary thoughts during prayer, but also of our most devout reflections and aspirations insofar as we treat them as indispensable means of going to God.

        Open Mind Open Heart p. 15

$\mathcal{A}$nything that we perceive of God can only be a radiance of His presence and not God as He is Himself. . . . There is nothing wrong with distinguishing different aspects of the Ultimate Mystery, but it would be a mistake to identify them with the inaccessible Light.

Open Mind Open Heart p. 17

So long as you *feel* united to God, it cannot be full union. So long as there is a thought, it is not full union. The moment of full union has no thought. You don't know about it until you emerge from it.

🏵 *Open Mind Open Heart p. 74*

*D*o not resist any thought, do not hang on to any thought, do not react emotionally to any thought. This is the proper response to all . . . kinds of thoughts that come down the stream of consciousness.

      Open Mind Open Heart p. 99

When you withdraw from your ordinary flow of superficial thoughts on a regular daily basis, you get a sharper perspective on your motivation and you begin to see that the value systems by which you have always lived have their roots in pre-rational attitudes that have never been honestly and fully confronted. . . . The emotional programs of early childhood that are buried in your unconscious begin to emerge into clear and stark awareness.

🪷 *Open Mind Open Heart p. 94*

*I*f we stop reflecting on ourselves, we will move into perfect peace. This innate tendency to be aware of oneself is the last stronghold of self-centeredness.

                  🪷 *Open Mind Open Heart p. 91*

$\mathcal{T}$he alternation between tranquillity and the struggle with thoughts is part of a process, a refining of the intuitive faculties so that they can be attentive to this deeper level in a more and more stable fashion.

Open Mind Open Heart p. 39

FOUR

The Human Condition

Contemplative prayer addresses the
human condition exactly where it is.

Invitation to Love p. 5

The spiritual journey is characterized by the ever-increasing knowledge of our mixed motivations, the dark sides of our personalities, and the emotional traumas of early childhood.

         ❧ *Invitation to Love p. 67*

$\mathcal{M}$ost of us have a heavy burden of emotional junk accumulated from early childhood. The body serves as the storehouse for this undigested emotional material. The Spirit initiates the process of healing by evacuating the junk. This takes place as a result of the deep rest of mind and body in contemplative prayer.

Invitation to Love p. 110

Lacking the experience of divine union, we feel alienated from ourselves, God, other people and the cosmos. Hence, we seek substitutes for the happiness for which we are predestined but which we do not know how to find.

🌸 *Open Mind Open Heart p. 5*

Self-knowledge in the Christian ascetical tradition is insight into our hidden motivation, into emotional needs and demands that are percolating inside of us and influencing our thinking, feeling, and activity without our being fully aware of them.

      Open Mind Open Heart p. 94

$\mathcal{N}$egative feelings toward oneself tend to be prevalent in our culture due to the low self-image people develop in early childhood, possibly because of our highly competitive society. Any one who does not win feels that he is no good in this culture, whereas in the quiet of deep prayer, you are a new person, or rather, you are you.

Open Mind Open Heart p. 65

$\mathcal{T}$he divine presence has always been with us, but we think it is absent. That thought is the monumental illusion of the human condition. The spiritual journey is designed to heal it.

❦ *Invitation to Love p. 90*

*I*n contemplative prayer the Spirit puts us in a position where we are at rest and disinclined to fight. By his secret anointing the Spirit heals the wounds of our fragile human nature at a level beyond our psychological perception, just as a person who is anesthetized has no idea of how the operation is going until after it is over.

❦ *Open Mind Open Heart p. 45*

When we work to surrender our own desires, world view, self-image, and all that goes to make up the false self, we are truly participating in Christ's emptying of himself.

Heart of the World p. 22

$\mathcal{T}$he spiritual journey is not a success story, but a series of diminutions of self. Saint Bernard of Clairvaux, the twelfth century Cistercian abbot, taught that humiliation is the path to humility.

Invitation to Love p. 97

$\mathcal{P}$ersonal sin is the refusal to respond to Christ's self-communication. (grace) It is the deliberate neglect of our own genuine needs and those of others.

       🕮 *Open Mind Open Heart p. 129*

$\mathcal{T}$he attraction to let go of spiritual consolation in order to let God act with complete freedom is the persistent attraction of the Spirit. The more one lets go, the stronger the presence of the Spirit becomes.

🪷 *Open Mind Open Heart p. 17*

Nothing is more helpful to reduce pride than the actual experience of self-knowledge. If we are discouraged by it, we have misunderstood its meaning.

Invitation to Love p. 67

[God] will bring people and events into our lives, and whatever we may think about them, they are designed for the evolution of his life in us.

Heart of the World p. 41

$\mathcal{T}$he reason any expectation is a hindrance is that it is a form of clinging, hence a desire to control.

Open Mind Open Heart p. 76

$\mathcal{M}$ost of our troubles come from expectations that are unrealistic and cannot be fulfilled.

                        Invitation to Love p. 118

· FIVE ·

Crisis

Suffering is part of the warp and woof of living. It is not an end in itself, but part of the price one has to pay for being greatly loved. Love, whether human or divine, makes you vulnerable.

❦ *Open Mind Open Heart p. 77*

Vulnerability means to be hurt over and over again without seeking to love less, but more.

$\mathcal{F}$ailure is the path to boundless confidence in God. Always remember that you have a billion chances.

🪷 *Open Mind Open Heart p. 74*

*H*umility is an attitude of honesty with God, oneself, and all of reality. It enables us to be at peace in the presence of our powerlessness and to rest in the forgetfulness of self.

Open Mind Open Heart p. 132

$\mathcal{D}$etachment is the goal of self-denial. It is the non-possessive attitude toward all of reality, the disposition that strikes at the root of the false self system. The false self is a monumental illusion, a load of habitual thinking patterns and emotional routines that are stored in the brain and nervous system.

        ❦ *Open Mind Open Heart p. 16*

We must try to perceive Christ in the interruption of our plans and in the disappointment of our expectations; in difficulties, contradictions, and trials. No matter what happens, *"We know that in everything God works for good with those who love him"* *(Rom. 8:28).*

Heart of the World p. 41

*T*his is the disposition God waits for in the crisis of faith: trust in His mercy no matter what kind of treatment He gives you. Only great faith can penetrate those apparent rebuffs, comprehend the love which inspires them, and totally surrender to it.

      🪷 *Crisis of Faith, Crisis of Love p. 29*

*F*rom the point of view of divine love, pain can be joy. It is a way of sacrificing ourselves completely for the sake of the Beloved. It does not cease to be pain, but it has a different quality from ordinary pain.

Open Mind Open Heart p. 77

$\mathcal{S}$uffering and death are not enemies,

but doors leading to new levels

of knowledge and of love.

                          Heart of the World p. 19

God holds back his infinite mercy from rushing to the rescue when we are in temptation and difficulties. He will not actively intervene because the struggle is opening and preparing every recess of our being for the divine energy of grace. God is transforming us so that we can enjoy the divine life to the full once it has been established. If the divine help comes too soon before the work of purification and healing has been accomplished, it may frustrate our ultimate ability to live the divine life.

Invitation to Love p. 82

· SIX ·

Faith

When faith grows into confidence, the crisis of faith has done its work and the crisis itself is resolved. Deep interior peace reigns.

🕮 *Crisis of Faith, Crisis of Love p. 32*

$\mathcal{T}$he way of pure faith is to persevere in contemplative practice without worrying about where we are on the journey, and without comparing ourselves with others or judging others' gifts as better than ours. . . . In pure faith, the results are often hidden even from those who are growing the most.

         ❧ *Invitation to Love p. 118*

$\mathcal{F}$aith calls for the total surrender of our faculties and of all our being to the truth inside and outside ourselves.

❦ Heart of the World p. 40

$\mathcal{A}$s soon as we begin to want to see and understand, or to depend on concepts or feelings to go to God, we withdraw from faith.

❦ *Heart of the World p. 40*

God helps us to disidentify from our preconceived ideas by enlightening us from within by the contemplative gifts of the Spirit. Through the infusion of his light and the assurance of his love, he lets us in on our weaknesses and deficiencies—not to overwhelm us with discouragement, but to encourage us to entrust ourselves completely to his infinite mercy.

Invitation to Love p. 70

Seek Him for His sensible presence, and
He hides. Seek Him by faith, that is, for
Himself, and you will find Him.

         Crisis of Faith, Crisis of Love p. 47

$\mathcal{F}$aith alone can perceive God triumphing
in the midst of human suffering and
bringing about the reign of divine love.

ঙ *Heart of the World p. 19*

$\mathcal{T}$he divine light of faith is totally available in the degree that we consent and surrender ourselves to its presence and action within us. It heals the wounds of a lifetime and brings us to transforming union, empowering us to enter Christ's redemptive program, first by the healing of our own deep wounds, and then by sharing in the healing of others.

Invitation to Love p. 119

· SEVEN ·

Transforming
Union,
Divine Energy

$\mathcal{T}$ransforming union is a restructuring of consciousness, not an experience or set of experiences.

🪷 *Invitation to Love p. 93*

The tendency of the transforming union as an abiding state is rather to be without extraordinary experiences and to lead ordinary daily life in an unobtrusive way. . . . One is completely free of the results and does not draw one's identity from any glamorous role, but is simply, like God, the servant of creation.

Invitation to Love p. 111

*I*n divine union, the great "I" of Jesus Christ becomes our "I." Our identity becomes rooted in him rather than in our own interests. If we still have interests, we are ready to give them up at the request of the Spirit. . . .

         Invitation to Love p. 111

$\mathcal{T}$he divine energy in itself is infinite potentiality and actuality. Creatures are localized manifestations of it. If there is no obstacle in us, no false self, we become transmitters through whom the divine presence as boundless love and compassion communicates itself to others in ever widening circles of influence.

❦ *Invitation to Love p. 102*

Divine love triumphs over every obstacle, including suffering and death.

❦ *Heart of the World p. 21*

Transforming union is the ripe fruit of dismantling the false self. As soon as the false self is reduced to zero, transforming union occurs. A nonpossessive attitude toward everything, including ourselves, is established because there is no longer a self-centered "I" to possess anything. This does not mean that we do not use the good things of life, but now they are not ends in themselves but stepping-stones to God's presence. . . . What is true, beautiful, and good in everything that exists becomes transparent.

          Invitation to Love p. 102

Transforming union is not a free ticket to happiness in this world. For some, this may mean a life of complete solitude full of loneliness; for others, it may mean an active apostolate that prevents them from enjoying the delights of divine union; for others again, it may mean intense suffering—physical, mental or spiritual— which they undergo for some special intention or for the whole human family.

Open Mind Open Heart p. 105

*H*uman effort depends on grace even as it invites it. Whatever degree of divine union we may reach bears no proportion to our effort. It is the sheer gift of divine love.

            Open Mind Open Heart p. 132

Service without seeking any return characterizes the Ultimate Reality. Those in transforming union are beginning to find that out. Hence, they too become servants, not dominators.

Invitation to Love p. 103

The night of sense enables us to perceive that the source of the emotional programs for happiness is selfishness. By letting go our desires for satisfaction in these areas, we move toward a permanent disposition of peace. Upsetting thoughts and emotions arise, but they no longer build up into emotional binges. The immense energy that was required to bear the afflictive emotions . . . is now available for more useful things, such as loving the people with whom we live and whom we are trying to serve.

               Invitation to Love p. 76

*D*ivine union is the goal of all Christians. We have been baptized; we receive the Eucharist; we have all the necessary means of growing as human beings and as children of God. It is a mistake to think that a special state of life is the only way of doing it.

🪷 *Open Mind Open Heart p. 33*

$\mathcal{T}$he love of Christ manifested itself in his sheer vulnerability. The crucifix is the sign and expression of the total vulnerability of Jesus: the out-stretched arms, the open heart, the forgiveness of everything and everyone. This sheer vulnerability made him wide open both to suffering *and* to joy.

      Heart of the World p. 13

Grace is the presence and action of
Christic at every moment of our lives.

                 ❦ *Open Mind Open Heart p. 128*

*H*appiness can be found only in the experience of union with God, the experience that also unites us to everyone else in the human family and to all reality.

Open Mind Open Heart p. 5

$\mathcal{D}$ivine love is compassionate, tender, luminous, totally self-giving; seeking no reward, unifying everything.

Open Mind Open Heart p. 129

$\mathcal{T}$he best way to receive divine love is to give it away, and the more we pass on, the more we increase our capacity to receive.

         Heart of the World p. 15

Our capacity for the transcendent is precisely what distinguishes us most from the rest of visible creation. It is what makes us most human.

⚘ *Heart of the World p.* 7

$\mathcal{T}$he fundamental purpose of prayer,
including the prayer of petition, is not to
get something from God, or to change
God, but to change ourselves. When we
have changed, God can give us everything
we want, because our will will be one with
his, and we will want only what he wants.

⚘ *Heart of the World p. 63*

EIGHT

Interior Silence

Silence is God's first language; everything else is a poor translation. In order to hear that language, we must learn to be still and to rest in God.

Invitation to Love p. 90

*N*ature seems to have provided us with the need of interior silence. We seek it as we seek returning to a place of security, warmth and love.

Heart of the World p. 9

This Presence is immense, yet so humble; awe-inspiring, yet so gentle; limitless, yet so intimate, tender and personal. . . . This Presence is healing, strengthening, refreshing. . . . A door opens within me, but from the other side. I seem to have tasted before the mysterious sweetness of this enveloping, permeating Presence. It is both emptiness and fullness at once.

Open Mind Open Heart p. 137

*T*he most effective silence takes place
when one is not even aware of being
silent . . .

🪷 *Heart of the World p. 65*

We wait patiently; in silence, openness, and quiet expectancy; motionless within and without. We surrender to the attraction to be still, to be loved, just to be.

        ❧ *Open Mind Open Heart p. 137*

Once we are thoroughy established in interior silence, it accompanies or pursues us through our daily routine. While conversations with God on other levels will still arise spontaneously, interior silence is the essential conversation.

Heart of the World p. 58

*I*nterior silence is one of the most strengthening and affirming of human experiences. There is nothing more affirming, in fact, than the experience of God's presence. That revelation says as nothing else can, "You are a good person. I created you and I love you."

      🌻 *Open Mind Open Heart p. 66*

$\mathcal{A}$ commitment to the contemplative dimension of the Gospel is the keystone to accepting the guidance of the Holy Spirit both in prayer and in action.

Invitation to Love p. 130

When you are being constantly reaffirmed by the presence of God in deep silence, you are not afraid of being contradicted or imposed upon. You might be humble enough to learn something from insults and humiliations without being overwhelmed by feelings of self-depreciation or revenge.

Open Mind Open Heart p. 65

$\mathcal{T}$he interior experience of God's presence activates our capacity to perceive Him in everything else—in people, in events, in nature.

❧ *Open Mind Open Heart p. 44*

Total response to Christ is only possible
when we hear his word on every level of
our being, including the deepest level,
which is that of interior silence.

Heart of the World p. 32

The Spirit speaks to our conscience through scripture and through the events of daily life. Reflection on these two sources of personal encounter and the dismantling of the emotional programming of the past prepare the psyche to listen at more refined levels of attention. The Spirit then begins to address our conscience from that deep source within us which is our true Self. This is contemplation properly so-called.

⚘ *Open Mind Open Heart p. 17*

The Holy Spirit inspired those who wrote the scriptures. He is also in our hearts inspiring us and teaching us how to read and listen. When these two inspirations fuse, we really understand what scripture is saying; or at least we understand what God at this moment is saying to us through it.

      ❦ *Heart of the World p. 47*

*I*nterior silence is the perfect seed bed for divine love to take root. In the Gospel the Lord speaks about a mustard seed as a symbol of divine love. It is the smallest of all seeds, but it has an enormous capacity for growth. Divine love has the power to grow and transform us. The purpose of contemplative prayer is to facilitate the process of inner transformation.

Open Mind Open Heart p. 45

Service

Service is the hallmark of one who is sent by God. The true prophet, martyr, spiritual leader, or teacher does not try to dominate others.

🌸 *Invitation to Love p. 96*

*I*nterior experience is geared to action. It is designed to soften up our self-centered dispositions, to deliver us from what is compulsive in our motivation, and to open us up completely to God and to the genuine service of others.

Heart of the World p. 13

One cannot be a Christian without social concern. There is no reason why anyone should go hungry even for a day. Since the resources are there, why do millions continue to starve? The answer must be greed.

❦ *Invitation to Love p. 125*

Contemplative prayer is a preparation for action, for action that emerges from the inspiration of the Spirit in the silencing of our own agitation, desires and hang-ups. Such silence gives God the maximum opportunity to speak.

❦ *Open Mind Open Heart p. 64*

$\mathcal{T}$he contemplative state is established when contemplative prayer moves from being an experience or series of experiences to an abiding state of consciousness. The contemplative state enables one to rest and act at the same time because one is rooted in the source of both rest and action.

Open Mind Open Heart p. 75

$\mathcal{A}$n important part of the response to divine love, once it has been received, is to pass it on to our neighbor in a way that is appropriate in the present moment.

Open Mind Open Heart p. 103

$\mathcal{A}$s the relationship of intimacy with God begins to deepen, you should not unduly prolong your time of prayer. When there is some duty to be performed, you have to sacrifice for the moment your attraction to interior silence.

     Open Mind Open Heart p. 77

$\mathcal{T}$he failure of our efforts to serve teaches us how to serve: that is, with complete dependence on divine inspiration. This is what changes the world.

                      ❦ *Invitation to Love p. 129*

$\mathcal{T}$he habit of service to others is developed by trying to please God in what we do and by exercising compassion for others, beginning with those with whom we live.

❧ *Open Mind Open Heart p. 16*

$\mathcal{S}$olitude is not primarily a place, but an attitude of total commitment to God. When one belongs completely to God, the sharing of one's life and gifts continually increases.

Open Mind Open Heart p. 131

*I*t is not so much what we do but what we *are* that allows God to live in the world. When the presence of God emerges from our inmost being into our faculties, whether we walk down the street or drink a cup of soup, divine life is pouring into the world.

🪷 *Open Mind Open Heart p. 63*

W_e have the obligation to pass on the environment intact to the next generation. We are only brief sojourners on this planet and must consider what happens after we are gone.

🕮 *Invitation to Love p. 125*

· TEN ·

From the Gospel –Scriptural Foundation

Peace is the great gift of Jesus on the day of his resurrection. The peace that Jesus offers is not sentimental. This peace transcends joy and sorrow, hope and despair. This peace is rooted in a way of being that transcends the emotions.

🕮 *Invitation to Love p. 111*

$\mathcal{T}$he grace of Christmas is to know Christ in his humanity. The grace of Epiphany is to know him in his divinity. The grace of Holy Week is to know him in his emptying and dying. The grace of Easter is to know him in his triumph over sin and death. And the grace of the Ascension is to know him in the whole of his being, as the Cosmic Christ. It is to know the glorified Christ, who passed, not into some geographical location, but into the depths of all creation.

               ✿ *Heart of the World p. 74*

The grace of the ascension enables us to perceive the irresistible power of the Spirit transforming everything into Christ despite any and all appearances to the contrary. In the misery of the ghetto, the battlefield, the concentration camp; in the family torn by dissension; in the loneliness of the orphanage, old-age home, or hospital ward . . . the light of the ascension is burning with irresistible power. This is one of the greatest intuitions of faith.

Heart of the World p. 73

$\mathcal{T}$he poor in spirit are those who accept afflictions for God's sake. They are not only the materially poor, but also those who suffer any affliction, whether emotional, mental or physical, and who accept their situation out of love of God. The poor have a special claim on the kingdom because they literally do not have anything, or if they do have possessions, they are willing to let them go as the needs of others or the will of God may require.

Invitation to Love p. 105

$\mathcal{T}$he experience of happiness in the face of destitution, poverty, and affliction is the fruit of accepting what is. By accepting reality, we are free of our predetermined demands and shoulds. It is not just a passive acceptance, however. We may also be asked by God to do something to change, improve, or correct situations, including defending ourselves or others when circumstances call for it.

Invitation to Love p. 105

The beatitude "Happy are those who mourn, for they will be comforted" speaks to the exaggerated demand for affection/ esteem and pleasure. The refusal to let go of what is being taken from us creates tension. When we let go of some person, place or thing that we love, we automatically enter a period of mourning. If we accept the loss of what we loved, we experience freedom from what we formerly depended upon excessively and we enter into a new relationship with it, based on the new freedom that does not try to squeeze absolute happiness from passing pleasures.

Invitation to Love p. 105

The third beatitude, "Happy are the meek," addresses the drive for power, as if to say "How happy you would be if you did not want to control situations, other people, or your own life, and if you possessed the freedom to accept insults and injustice without being blown away."

Invitation to Love 106

"*H*appy are the merciful, mercy will be shown to them" is the beatitude that corresponds to the full reflective self-consciousness of mental egoic consciousness. At this level we become fully human. Our response to life is cooperative, nonjudgemental, and accepting of others. This beatitude fulfills Christ's new commandment, "Love one another as I have loved you" (John 15:12)

          Invitation to Love p. 109

The beatitude "Happy are those who hunger and thirst for justice; they will have their fill" addresses over identification with our social group and frees us from the urgency to be accepted and approved by the group. In order to respond to the invitation of the gospel, we need to go beyond the behavior that may be held in honor or demanded by the particular social group to which we belong. . . . We have the freedom to remain within our tradition or institution while at the same time working for its renewal.

      ⚘ *Invitation to Love p. 107*

$\mathcal{T}$he beatitude that corresponds to the intuitive level is the beatitude of the pure of heart and the promise is, "They will see God." They will see him not with their bodily eyes, of course, but with the eyes of the spirit purified by faith.

                            ❦ *Invitation to Love p. 110*

To love one's neighbor as oneself is to respect the image of God in our neighbor with all the rights which that dignity confers. To love one another as Jesus loves us is to love one another in our humanness—in our individuality and opinionatedness, in personality conflicts and in unbearable situations. It is to continue to show love, no matter what the provocation may be to act otherwise.

Invitation to Love p. 109

*P*eople who injure us are doing us a great favor because they are providing us with the opportunity of passing on the mercy that we have received. By showing mercy, we increase the mercy we receive.

Heart of the World p. 14

*I*n the liturgy, eternal time penetrates each moment of chronological time. Eternal values breaking into chronological time are made available to us in the present moment.

❦ *Open Mind Open Heart p. 9*

*I*n seminaries today there is danger that the knowledge of theology and scripture may pass through the minds of the professors into the minds of the students without passing through the hearts of either. Unless it finds a place in their hearts, the message of the Gospel may be preached, but it is not going to be lived.

❧ *Heart of the World p. 45*

*L*ay people living quiet, prayerful lives in the world, who think they are not contemplative because they never became monks or nuns, and elderly religious, who think they are not contemplatives because of the misunderstandings about contemplative prayer in recent centuries, may be so holy that they are not even upset by their apparent failure as contemplatives. This is the triumph of hiddenness.

❦ *Invitation to Love p. 119*

One final word of caution is in order. While we may talk of the divine "plan" and outline the stages of the spiritual journey as presented by the great teachers of our tradition, the only thing we can be absolutely sure of in the spiritual journey is that whatever we are expecting to happen will not happen. God is not bound by our ideas. . . . One way or the other, we will have to take the leap of trust into the unknown.

         ❧ *Invitation to Love p. 100*